BEYOND THE WOUNDED HORIZON

by
J Lester Allen
and
James H Duncan

Beyond the Wounded Horizon © by J Lester Allen and James H Duncan, 2020.

All rights reserved. No part of this book may be reproduced in any form by any electronic or mechanical means including photocopying, recording, or information storage and retrieval without permission in writing from the author unless for critical reviews and articles.

Published by Alpine Ghost Press
ISBN: 978-0-578-69357-6
Cover design and front photo by James H Duncan

Acknowledgements

J Lester Allen would like to thank the following publications where some of these poems first appeared: *Opium Poetry*, *Rusty Truck*, *Trailer Park Quarterly, and The Chirion Review.* Other pieces appeared in the promotional chapbook *In Other Julys* (Inkstained Dagger Press, 2010).

James H Duncan would like to thank the following publications where some of these poems first appeared: *Plainsongs*, *Red Fez*, *Rural Messenger Press*, *Carcinogenic Poetry,* and *The Rye Whiskey Review*. Other pieces appeared in the now out-of-print chapbook *Maybe A Bird Will Sing* (Bird War Press, 2009).

"A time splashed with interest, wounded with tragedy, crevassed with joy—that's the time that seems long in the memory. Eventlessness has no post to drape duration on. From nothing to nothing is no time at all."

— John Steinbeck

J LESTER ALLEN

Healthy life choices to make by age 40
(for James Duncan)

sitting in a dive bar in
Rome, NY with a pint of the dark
stuff and a stout old friend, swapping stories
while waiting for the big poetry
show to begin. it had been years
since I found myself able to do it
but somehow this one felt right,
perhaps it was my phenomenal conditioning—
the intense cardio workouts
of late, improved breathing techniques
or maybe some sage old poet's vision
finally worming its way into the light,
from any angle the atmosphere was there
for a full-on firing squad assault,
you could almost smell the
gunpowder in the room, wafting out and
over the hushed jukebox, swirling
mad around the young professional couple
seated at the end of the bar, hanging out like a light
that you know is always on if
you just knew where to look,
as then more faces of friends
came in off the street
and handshakes and
raised glasses to old times,
at some point I turned back to the muted tv behind the bar—
Healthy Life Choices to Make by Age 40
flashed behind the news anchor
on the screen
I couldn't make out quite what she was saying,
but her angle on things seemed clear:
Eat more greens, her hips were suggesting, *though be careful
of the many chemicals*

*applied to them to keep
the beetles from taking over the
world, so wash them thoroughly or
eat organic ones instead. Exercise more
but avoid running, it's hard on the
joints, and sit-ups are
ill-advised, (all the fitness experts have confirmed this).
Drink less of course, though a glass of red wine a day is good
for your veins, your heart...*
except I had recently read that the throngs of experts are
divided over that one too...
are eggs in this year?
how about apples?
is frequent masturbation still
a good approach to fighting prostate
cancer?
I also heard that we'd be better off
absorbing the radiation when getting x-rays
or CAT scans than dressing our organs in those heavy lead
aprons...
no one seems to have any of
it figured.

the segment was cut off before
she got around to giving her
verdict on
poetry but looking around the room
I was pretty sure that
I had my answer.

I laid down the last of my money and
raised my empty up where the barkeep
could see it, figuring it best to get
back to things more
easily understood.

As ever as the dinosaurs

we are at the park when
a young girl runs past our blanket
an eternity of blond curls
sits atop her bobbing head.

she is chasing a bug, or perhaps a figment, either way
whatever it is seems
very real to her.

it is as real as an
octopus or an onion
fresh from it's skin, a fresh car
collision,

a tire iron
in the middle of
a road unseen
or
the mad, blowing
bugle of
everywhere.

I look at the darkening clouds directly overhead
and think about
how it could all come crashing down
at any
moment

but
doesn't.

Dear landlord
(For Roger Schnock)

dear landlord,

I know that wrinkled wad of paper
that I placed in your mailbox this
morning wouldn't pass for currency
even if this poem somehow gets me
famous, but I meant every
word and there's value in the truth,
wouldn't you agree?

dear landlord,

yes, I read the lease and no
those people in my place last
night were not my friends
and I did not authorize such debauchery
you see, I was too drunk
on brown liquor to authorize
much of anything,
while screaming the darkest parts
of my soul into
this borrowed plumbing.

dear landlord,

I promise, she will not be coming back.
what she had against my bookcase
and my coffee table is beyond
me, she's crazy,
certifiable, please let Jennifer downstairs know
there will be no more trouble out of 4B.

dear landlord,

yes, those were squad cars
on the street last night,
again
but they were here for that
malcontent next door pounding on the walls
shouting demands of the Gods
naked, then rolling around in the
yard screaming like a rabbit in a foxes'
jaw after I gave him one pint glass
of wine, and refused to let him
use my phone,

I did not know,

believe me.

dear landlord,

that piney, citrus
smell
emanating from the kitchen
cupboard isn't cat-piss
and it wasn't my
cat.

dear landlord,
I am going to be a few days late with
the rent again this month,
the bank fucked up. I
certainly wasn't playing
the penny stocks again,
right hand to
God.

dear landlord,

yes, that was me in my
underwear early this morning educating
the college kids upstairs
on neighborly etiquette after
them deciding that 1:30 am on a Tuesday
is prime time for an acoustic
Bruce Springsteen
singalong, no offense to
The Boss.

dear landlord,

no, that was not a raccoon in my
living room, I'll have your rent
by Wednesday.

dear landlord,

the clerk from the liquor store
across the street (did you know he's from Siberia?)
was not wrong when he described, in detail
my Saturday night to you. and yes, I am aware
that there are several small children in the
neighborhood…and yes, of course she is of legal age and no,
it won't happen
again.

dear landlord,

I really need that security deposit back,
that mirror in the bathroom
has always been cracked like
that and these
walls were blue when
I moved in here,
not the other way
around.

Hindsight

another one in
the books. I sit here
listening to a recording of
Elvis singing "Auld Lang Sine"
sipping at some prosecco
as the once cryptorchid
balls
of another year

d
r
o
p

into history.

The mountain
(for Dan Collins)

a motion picture was playing on
the TV—a boy who wasn't much older
than 16 was there on the screen
taking pictures of the insane
for the doctor who was rearranging the
thoughts of his patients
with electro-shock and other
more extreme procedures while
my pet opossum sauntered across the
dusty hardwood to give the cat a hard time as
Gene Autry sang *Home on the Range,*
now a very drunk and very French man was on set screaming
at anyone that would listen,
"Have you earned the glow?"
he asked madly of the boy from earlier and whom was very
much infatuated with
the man's daughter, who herself
was sleeping just
down the hall,
but the boy did not answer, seeming somewhat
terrified.

"I am the future!" the man said in his mother tongue,
"I know things…"

"je lie les atomes dans le ciel"

"I tie the atoms in the sky," he said, crazed
through a mad man's
tears.
then the film cut to a scene of the boy and the girl having
escaped her lunatic father,
driving high up

a mountain in a little blue car,
the snow heavier as they
went up,
quite under-dressed and
underprepared
for everything coming their way.
and then the screen
went black.

it reminded me of this one time I
found a car wrecked and still running in the woods—
it was Valentine's day 3 years ago and
ice age cold,
the driver's door was wide open,
a full grown Rottweiler sitting
in the passenger seat seeming most content
and a cockatoo
appearing quite oblivious
situated directly behind,
they were just hanging out there together like that—
two passengers on some ill-fated ride into
a cold hell.
the driver was up the road a short ways wearing only
a slip and her frostbitten skin
and the state trooper who got there
very soon after the series of missteps began said the woman
had been crazy for most of her
life and that she
probably wouldn't be coming back for the animals
anytime soon.

I look back at my opossum crawling towards me now
as the credits creep on and
can't help but wonder
what the weather
will be like
tomorrow.

B-13

we were
sitting there in the lobby of the
Oddfellow's old folks home,
my brother and I.
we couldn't have been much older
than 12 and 9,
laughing uncontrollably
at all the old
people groaning and
muttering strange, nonsensical things
one man kept running his walker into
the automatic doors,
which, in a nursing home are really just
magical metal walls that your loved ones
disappear into
unless you've got the
secret codes to
open them.
realizing this he began shouting
curse words that
my young ears had never heard
outside of late night soft-core
Cinemax movies,
and then
the nurses had to
take the walker away
and put him in
a chair, his face a helpless shade
of red in a palette of
defeat measured
against a time when doors
were not so definite.
then they wheeled
grandma out and

we all sat around her
asking her the most
depressing questions
about the food and
what happened to her
neighbor Mr. Walton,
who last we knew kept getting into trouble
because he would sleepwalk his way
into bed
with the other residents, uninvited,
but grandma
kept herself in good
spirits, talking to my brother and I
over our
immature laughter...
don't do that, she said. *someday*
you will be in here and then I
will do it to you.

I am still haunted by
that line.

then she made a joke
and said
she was looking
forward to bingo night
and winning it all
when
there was nothing
left for her to
lose.

Black car

the week began
on a Tuesday. I remember
the October sky,
the great beautiful bird of
eternity pulling people up into
the sun circling overhead,
like the last thing
a soul would ever see before
departing this world.
they pulled a body from
the campus creek, a Florida
boy now only a picture, a headline,
a pair of empty tennis shoes, and
somewhere a mother
and regrets.

the air is getting colder, they say.
it will be a bad winter, they say.
a lot of things are said
which maybe
should not be said—

I felt steel wheels upon
my brain then, like a cold
stethoscope hunting disease,
when dreaming
was still an acceptable way to pass
the time,
while warm windows burn
in a cold part of this town,
and a lonely pair of headlights chew
loudly
into the night.

Here in the afternoon

here in the afternoon
there is death in the refrigerator's hum
in whir of the hard-drive
in every trick of tick of clock

here in the afternoon
there is death in the kitchen
in a cage
in chimes of the doorbell
in the idle of an engine
in threatening rings of the telephone
where my heart nearly stops

here in the afternoon
there is death in distant traffic
in helicopters overhead
in leaf
blowers and
lawn
mowers
in the vacant growl of
my empty stomach

here in the afternoon
there are timidities in your voice
from behind a closed door
like a cat's claw
chasing mice through
my veins
an ambulance siren
sounds as
dogs bark at the ghosts of love

here in the afternoon

these walls sizzle like
bacon in a hot pan
like a baseball crowd
like 4th of July

the past stops by
to say hello, stopping
just long enough for me
to get a good whiff
of its cheap perfume

while dumping bottles of those
days like a stale
poison into my
brain,
watered down some
by time
but still possessing
that old familiar
sting.

He does not work here anymore

waiting patiently is defeat
in each and every rusty old mailbox
a defeat like death or madness slowly
sucking the life,
their displeased stares sharpen upon me
their bad breath showers down
like a curtain of no
curiosity while these
lifeless souls wait for the death-ringer to come
and collect them
one by one from the outworn
nothingness of their sleepy lives while
bitching about everything:

the fall has come too soon,
the sky is too blue,
have you been reading my
Playboys again?
when will you people start
getting here on time?

and children with their well-developed egos
and attitudes absorbed from their fathers
make me feel small,
unprepared
as the truck rocks back
and forth from the passing of
the large chicken haulers
flocking this town
maybe the next one will clip
my bumper and send me hurling through
the windshield
crashing down upon the spikes of
my own death

like a swarm of pestilence in the streets
with a breast of feathers
to hide the rotting of the
crows inside of me
but instead I wave and
waive,
smile through facade of
teeth,
attempt to somehow
appease those eternally
displeased

like some
tired old farmer waiting for
cows that he knows ain't
ever coming
home.

Lefty and the pimp

Walking through the isles
of the discount grocery store
fresh from the job thinking of
how best to quiet an inner hunger
as rockets lay waste in a desert
halfway around the world, launched by drones,
at the command of powerful militaries
controlled by madmen
mashing at big buttons
with their tiny hands.

I found myself comparing the prices
of instant mashed potatoes when the whole
operation suddenly caught fire—

"Hey man," a voice called out from the dairy section,
"you work for the SPCA?"

I turned to see two men standing in front
of the butter that looked like they just walked off the
set of a Cohen Brother's film, as odd and mismatched as any
two men you'd ever see.
The talking one was short, round like a propane tank with long
brown hair and disorderly goatee.
He was missing his right forearm all the way up to the elbow
and had the whole show dressed
in a white jean jacket with a mouth-full of worn down, un-
white old teeth that some addiction or another had very clearly
had their way with.

"I usta have me a dog." he said.

I glanced down at his stump with what must have been a look
of confusion,

"Oh, no no" he said laughing, "I got that dog because of this."
(he shook his stump at me), "I needed protection, you see."
"Doberman, was a great dog,
I know why they call them Pinchers too." he said. "This one
time we were walking down the road and this other dog came
out of nowhere man," (he began making chomping motions
with his hand)
"and man that other dog beat it quick, tail between his legs and
all, lemme tell ya."

"Very intelligent dogs." I told him.

About then his cohort chimed in sounding like Sam Elliott
were he miscast as a dysfunctional cyborg in a lost Terminator
movie, stuttering in some broken language that I couldn't
make out,
he was late-fifties and well over 6 feet tall,
dressed in a wide-brim brown hat
and bright purple trench with a purple leopard collar.
Individually, they were notable.
but together they were
as unforgettable as the sound of rain
on a rooftop, or your middle name.

I said so long to the motley duo, having no idea
that a few minutes after, I'd see them stuffing
an old white Econoline with their haul when
the short one called out,

"Hey guy, come check this out!"

He moved to the back of the van when he split the rear doors
and stepped aside. I hesitantly approached to
find the thing stuffed full of boxes, made for TV this, 2 a.m.
infomercial that, it looked like these two
deranged cowboys had hijacked
a Shop at Home caravan on their way into town.

I peered at the mess in a hazy indifference.

"You fellas ought to start a business." I told him. "There's a lot going on here."

It wasn't that I thought anyone would actually
want any of the shit haphazardly jammed into that
old van, no, but because their brand of madness was
undoubtedly a marketable commodity,
they just needed to find the right buyer.

I wished the two well for a second time,
got into the car and pulled out of that parking lot
an indomitable mess of
twilight, powdered potatoes,
amusement
and
disbelief.

The sidewalk girls

not too good with eyes,
I must admit to
getting along much better
with the backs and behinds
of arch and sway,
the truthful tone of calves,
and beautiful ankles of
a better world.

the eyes want too much,
I can't bring myself to tell them
that they've been beaten
to the haul
and what remains
might not be worth the
price of admission.

so these blue eyes of
many things find themselves behind
sunglasses and
beneath ball caps,
submerged in cheap
liquor,

running from no
job, a wife in another
state, a life
just gone.

sometimes it takes a man
10 years to be
sure of what he knew
all along:

that the worm will always
get its apple, no matter
the season,
and that a summer
dress and stiff shot
of breeze, in all its
perennial beauty,
will never last any of us
quite long enough.

In lieu of the womb

give me the peace
of a rainy day in a
parked car,
give me a cat stretched out
in the sun forever,
give me the dark
loneliness of a
dive bar,
the raw excitement of
the ballpark,
the octagon.
give me the banging of
keys and of ice cubes
in the glass,
give me a tract of woods
a thousand miles wide,
a hot bath and a
cold beer.
give me an old movie
with Newman or Brando
or a Herman Raucher novel,
give me a park bench
with a sad-eyed stranger on the
other end,
a warm bed with a
close and loving friend.
give me a three-legged
dog, or a mountain top
in the clouds,

give me no politicians.

give me a stick of dynamite
thrown over a waterfall,

an afternoon that never
ends, give me
old friends and
new friends to
raise glasses with
in
honor of our
escaping.

The idiot tax

they never tell you how it's
going to be back when
you're first shot from
the gun—
having landed in grade-school mathematics class
all preoccupied with Tommy and how fast his train
is going if he's sitting next to a
blue orangutan on his way to his aunt's house holding
4 apples, and his tiny pecker.
then one day it hits you at the age of 13 or
30 or 55 or whenever it feels
like hitting you as you drive to a gas station that's 4 miles
further away
than some other station all to save 6 cents a gallon,
or stopping at 3 stores to buy
cheap avocados—an hour of life gone for .14 cents.
you'll adjust, eventually; their base-level tricks will
cease to fool you and yet, you will still be fooled by other
things—
failing to keep a tire iron handy after
you've already had the wheels roll away
on you once, that's the idiot tax,
paying bills late
habitually,
ignoring tooth pain, believing her
when she says "everything is fine"
after you find some other sucker's
ball cap on the back seat of her car,
that's the idiot tax.
free-trials, extended warranties, bullshit diets, penny stocks,
political swear-to-Gods, rental car
insurance,
people on dating websites who say, shortly before going to
bed with you—

I never do this kind of thing, it's just not my style, but YOU, YOU'RE different.

antibiotics are expensive…

also known as the idiot tax.

light beer, the lottery,
giving some poor homeless guy a buck
only to see him two days later
wearing a freshly pressed suit and
betting on a game of Blackjack,
that's when you know
they've got you.

I've decided, from here on out
to be smarter, I'm going to buy in bulk,
invest in this crypto-currency I keep
hearing so much about,
clip coupons and save all of
my receipts,
this life game is expensive
enough

even for those
who think they've got
the whole thing
figured.

A hole in many

legs unfold
beautifully toned and
glazed in a summer
bronze.

I see in their many movements
the rise of civilizations,
the reason for all war—
coins of thought
clinking in the
expired parking meter
of my brain, sitting here
with these strange
creatures on this strange couch
and I can't even remember how I got
here to begin with.

when at that moment, the door opens
and the apartment fills some more
with a large cast
of sharp-threaded, dull-
headed,
sculpted hair club-
hoppers,

I escape to the rooftop just
in time,
am offered a cigarette
by a pretty blond girl.
we talk a bit about
the night air and this new bar
across town that neither of us had
yet been to, as a guy emerges
from the apartment with a

bag of golf balls and a
club,
we took turns launching
those little white
soldiers through the windows
of the abandoned office
building across the
street,
laughing like the giddy and drunk children
that we were.

we did that for awhile then went
back inside,
the place had cleared out
except for the scraggly old calico
who had proudly reclaimed her couch
and a few traces of coke still
scattered on the
glass coffee table that
filled-in admirably for a 6am
cup of coffee.

the sun was coming up
and the morning with it
standing there, like a cross-
armed parent of no pleasing, asking me
what I was doing with
my life, and where the
hell had I left
the car.

Falling in my dreams

I have carved you from old
memories,
draped in torn bed-
sheets.
I found your scent in the
bar of soap next to
the sink; the girl in the
elevator looked through
me with your eyes
tonight,
the woman on the
TV news speaks your voice
through her lips
and smiles

I reach back through
a million instances—
broken down nightmares,
cars on fire in a vacant
lot of dreams,
memories I junked
years ago
resurrected now
in hopes of somehow
bringing you back
to me,

and standing before me
now, I can almost
touch you,
I can almost feel your breath
and taste your lips
upon mine
and feel the sweet

softness of your skin
upon my skin as the
worms make for the
light

but the past is nothing
if not a cruel joke
and tomorrow will be another
in a long parade of bad
punchlines

and when the sun
burglarizing my morning
through rented curtains becomes
too much and the voices
in the hall and
pounding on my door
become too much
it will be Tuesday
and every other damn thing
besides.

In our old age

it will come
like the sun
climbing the ladder of
a rose,
like the wax of the
moon or silent derision
of Columbus's compass

morning, a rock
through the window
or spoiled pear still
clinging to trees that
wave summer away

the millions of tiny
ant-like smiles that seep
from the seconds as skeletons
swim the seas of a
soft flesh

and the eyes,
eyes that still move with
a glistening wonder
tunnel through you,
like rockets in reverse,
their cauterized wounds
left behind and
those few holes,
the ones that won't ever close,
let the sunlight in
but just a little bit
just enough to remind you
that after all these
years you will still

know less than nothing

thankfully, there's
nothing to know
anyway.

The in-between

a quiet day
free of the rat-a-tat of the office
line breaking up
the silence, outside my
window I see
winter holding on
tightly like the talons
of an owl to its prey, as I
inside clutch firmly
to the winter of
myself.

the distant branches are
sheathed in ice,
there's a stillness
like after the dropping
of some big bomb
the air is as quiet
too, except for
one lonely crow
sitting high
atop a row
of telephone
poles
wondering perhaps
a great many
things or maybe thinking only:

*goddamn it is cold up
here.*

beneath his black
crow feathers inside
his black crow

head.

I see the truth of spinal
chords seated within speeding
machines, licking
at the salty pavement
as they go…
there is never enough
time and also
too much, so we
rush rush like
electricity humming
through walls
to the outlet
of home, of spring
of Fridays—
freedom, choice,
leisure &
love giving way
once again to
obligation, disappointment,
Mondays of frustration, failing health
and the rest,
and in-between there somewhere
is the
life, the most damned
beautiful, amazing thing
that there ever
was just waiting,
just waiting
for the cold to go
for some sun of a seasonal
mood,
for the world to be just
a little bit better
than it was.

hold on crow,
hold on.

The way the rain falls around here

she looked like
royalty standing in
the sun in her jeans
and high-heeled boots—

like some kind of highway
queen, awaiting the next
chapter.

the coyotes around here
cry a familiar song,
their hunger so
palpable it could
knock the wind
right out of
you.

Long odds

sometimes we
think that we
are truly unstoppable
that no disease or
circumstance or
traffic light
or flat tire or
inflated ego
could ever do us in.
we are wrong, of course,
we are always wrong.
even when we are right,
it is only because not enough
time has passed or
the lighting is not
so good—some thing looks
like something else,
a dusty shoe in
the back of a closet
in the shape of some distant
adolescent fear.
I read about a man on the internet,
a man who
jumped rope for
30 hours straight,
it made me want to end it all
to escape the
reality that this
is the way of the
world when it's
bent over and looking for
a nickel in the
rain,

that we even are
at all, most days,
is a miracle.

I look at my cat
sitting upright
like a little person.
he's licking where his
balls used to be
and I think
that the best of us
on the best of days
are still caught in
it, feeling around
in the dark with a
pair of sunglasses on
searching for
a knife to end our
suffering but finding
pacifiers and
inspirational quotes
written on the backs
of napkins
instead…

hold on friend,
you've got this,
no time like the present…
to finally plunge that
shiny knife into
that bleeding
unassailable
heart.

In other Julys

a rising heat bare-
footed walks,
a thistle moans
bare-chested
tousled hair
glint of eyes,

a boy on the
sidewalk with
flat basketball
looking most alone
or two old cats sprawled
on red steps as
the sun goes
down and you,
you blue and unnamed
sitting quietly in
the park with your legs,
your legs wrapped around
the moon,

while far-off stars
break bread with
the early evening
sky.

Lightning going by
(for Chris M.)

I remember riding
stolen bikes
through the
ghetto at 2am
for a score,
your soul a blaze
even then.

I saw a picture
of your little girl
on social media
yesterday. she's got
your eyes, your
smile and
those same crazy
curls.

you'd be so proud.

I miss you friend,

I'm glad you
burned for
as long
as you
did.

In the garage

the sockets and wrenches
      make fools,
I can still hear my father's voice

other left
other left
YOUR OTHER LEFT!

suffice to say
I don't spend much time there
these days and
it isn't because I feel like
a child in a man's place

no

that could be most anywhere,

but frankly

I'd rather be writing poems that
sometimes work instead of
wrenching on cars that
did until I started in on them—

if I ever do have kids,

I hope that they view poetry
differently.

Non-perishable

it's Sunday
there have been two deaths
in my house so far today
both carpenter ants
that my girlfriend stepped on.
one died instantly
the other,
just mangled enough
for us to be pressed into making
a decision.

there's a virus
running around the world
right now
that doesn't seem like much
but it has managed to
kill the stock
market so, that's something.
2% death rate is what they're
saying, 2
percent.
if you told me that I had a
two percent chance
of just about anything
I'd probably immediately lose interest
in whatever was to
follow but here
we are,
huddled together like
two helpless voles and
the fox is closing in,
we should probably
eat the last of
our fancy food and

drink the good beer
before the speculators
come to feast
on our
bones.

A letter from a future age

this seems like
a futile act.
a triviality based
on the odds
alone,
I realize,
but I thought
you should know—
if there's still a
moon in the night
sky, listen alright?

then there are likely
still fish in the rivers,
snails
within the sea, you
dig?
a chance is what I am
arriving at, do you understand?

pick up the phone or plug yourself in if there's
still a hum,
whatever you've
got to do,
find a pen, or even blood,
some
implement of
eternity
(we're damn fools aren't we?)
and try,
the worst thing
that could happen
is nothing
at all

(the best thing also.)

A goddamn sandwich

*Goddamn, look at the
size of that thing!* Tom said
pointing to the large spider
crawling across the porch
and beneath an empty
planter.

*I don't know how you sleep
with all these wolf spiders
crawling all over the place.*

*I'm much more concerned with
the neighbors at the end
of the street crawling all over
the place, I told him. Saw one of
them last week, stoned and shirtless in
the rain
walking off with a handful of
firewood.*

*I thought about chasing him
down but it didn't seem worth
it. I did load the boom-stick
for the next time though,*
I said with a silly wink.
*probably never use it anyway
but it's piece of mind in
these crazy times.*

Goddamn right, crazy, Tom said.
*You hear they closed all the
non-essential businesses
downtown? All the bars and
restaurants, the book stores.*

*Then this week they closed
the parks, the boat landings,
hell even the golf courses.*

The golf courses! he said.
*Pretty much everything but the
grocery and liquor stores.*

*Well that's good, at least they didn't
close those, there'd be real upheaval,
madness in the streets, for sure,* I said.

*I just don't know what everybody
is going to do,* he said. *We
weren't built for this.*

I guess everyone will just have to
sit around drinking, watching that
show about that tiger guy
and really getting to
know themselves…

I can't imagine it
going very well.

Dip shit apocalypse

standing in a grocery
line that wraps half-way
around the world—
tightly clutched carts full of Campbell's Chunky Soup
and Spaghetti-Os, all the bottles of
hand-sanitizer that a reusable
shopping bag can hold.
a woman with two carts of
toilet paper, believing apparently
that the end will be marked
by one big river of shit—
looking around I'm beginning
to think
she just might
be right.
it's the end of the world
as we know it and I too
feel an unsettling rumble
in my guts,
but if the 5G believers are to
be trusted all we need to do is
burn down the cell
towers,
who needs data anyway
in this new world
personality
disorder?
everyone knows that we're just a
hunch and three feelings away
from this thing disappearing
like a miracle on
Pennsylvania Ave.
And if that doesn't work
we've got Dr. Fauci to

hold gloved hands with as
we do-si-do through
the last song of civilization's
soundtrack,
or at least until a vaccine is
developed that Bill Gates
can shoe-horn a
microchip
into.
when they tally up
the dead
let's not forget, this virus
claimed the lives of
science
and civility once and for all.
common sense was
already scared into hiding, riding off
like an N-95 masked bandit
for the hills
it would all almost seem
like some weird
end-times dream, except
they say you can't read
while you're sleeping and
I've seen enough
CNN & Fox News headlines to
remind me
that you can lead The 4 Horsemen of
the Apocalypse to
The Kool Aid but you can't make them…
wait,
nevermind…

A very strange afternoon

lying in a rented
bed in a motor lodge room
of 1975 forever,
she rolls off of me
after fucking
me on the anniversary
of our love.

we lay there drinking
warm beer from the
can, I take a few drags
from the joint on the nightstand
and slowly sink into
the sunflower quilt
that is still neatly draped
over the old concrete slab
of mattress
when suddenly, a large
mass begins emerging from the ribs of
my chest, a large moss-covered rock,
a mountain begins
to grow from inside of me
somewhere.
a mountain of corduroy and
lavender, a mountain of old
baseball cards,
my first kiss,
the last words my friend Brad
said to me before he died
in a Cuban Jungle,
the time I got stung
by 100 bees and spent the afternoon
lying in my neighbor's basement
covered in toothpaste because his nurse mother

said it would draw the poison out.
I slowly roll the moss away
as my mountain begins to laugh,
its laugh rumbles
like a box of distant horse
sounds, as the room fills
with water,
fills my lungs as a
childhood picture of her that I had
never seen floats
by, as a canoe full of
caricaturized past Presidents floats
by pointing,
mocking, not helping me.
as my mountain grows taller
until its breaking apart
the tiles of the drop ceiling,
snapping the rafters,
growing towards the sky,
and blotting out the sun.
it was all most terrifying,
and as I lay there
in the rushing water
my mountain keeps
growing, taking the lodge
and the parking lot
and the club with the over-priced drinks
down the street with it.
there were motorcycle
sounds that seemed to stick
to the sides of my mountain
as it grew, gruff voices of men were
carried away by large-winged
birds. I turn to look
for her but she
is not there,
there is only tall green plants surrounding

the bed like something
from the Amazon
and the carcass of a large,
dead beetle and then
I hear more water sounds,
more water sounds,
her voice calling out
to me over the torrent—

You have the power to be something great!

What? I yell back into the abyss.

You have the power to be something great! she shouts out
again.

The power to what? Be what? I call out.

You have to shower, we're going to be late!
What are you doing in there?

at once the water subsided, the plants shriveled
down and away
the roof tiles snapped back into their
places. I felt my chest,
counted my ribs carefully,
pulled back the thick curtain and peered
out at the late
afternoon sun.

as I did, a small black beetle was
working his way up the
window,

I'm coming baby.
Leave the water on.

James H Duncan

Adrift a sea of ordinary laughter

even the bums there seemed jazz enlightened
standing along the Nashville downtown like doormen
for the blues bars and pool hall backrooms
where smoke and beer cast grisaille paintings
against our souls in sweet sad October, love waning
to a new moon darkness, true but no longer felt,
pool cues clicking adrift a sea of ordinary laughter,
money flailing from our pockets like dead
fish in this no oxygen air, this shifting sorrowful air
hanging heavy with our unspoken hopes that tomorrow
will not find us broke and devastated, though somehow
we should have known our spirits could only fly
so long without wings, so far without eyes,
and the tramp there who we saw outside panhandling
now comes down the rows of pool tables
begging for quarters and he comes to
us and we give him all we have,
the last of all we have, so little, so true,
and he moves on with a joke, to another
bar next door with hopes of quarters and cheap beer,
but not us, not now, so far from home in either direction
wandering blindly back down Nashville streets
looking at Nashville stars through Nashville
clouds never wanting sleep again for fear
of what dreams may come, but soon finding
that even that wish will fail us too
as the beer-rush thumping of our hearts
rocks our weary sadness into the final sleep
of our long gone youth

Ablution

standing alone
so far from home with the crickets

the stars throw
me off, but only for a blink
or two until
my mind realigns
with the darkness in the dark
the beating in the heart
the great strain and joy
of turning away
down
further
into the side of my mind
that never sees
the sun or the moon
the universal
maw of everything we don't know
about our human selves

finding solace in solitude is as
easy as sweeping the front
stoop free of unbroken rain

smile at the work, the broom
beats loudly tonight

Between piano songs

whiskey glasses
shatter in our last hurrah,
they stand so tall when empty,
so short when full,
just another ice-filled bottom
looking back up at not much
surrounded by not much
all dressed up like a gentleman tramp
like a rain-washed sidewalk
before the parade

I reach to pay for another as
lint and change rattle from the pocket
and only I know that the tip jar
right over there has more money
inside than I've seen in weeks

a pausing quiet between piano songs
sweeps up the broken moment
leaving the counter clean for more ash,
for more ring-soaked napkins,
for not much surrounded by not much

thinking about the day and all we lost
within it, it makes the eyes drop down
to the floor under my feet, cracked linoleum,
and I can't pull the eyes back up, thinking
suddenly how the stool beneath me was once a tree
like the drunk above it was once a man,
and how nobody knows my sorrows
save for the pause between piano songs
which never last for long

A man of himself
(for J Lester Allen)

you don't feign to know
you piecemeal the day from the floor of a house
you are rebuilding alone outside Harrisburg
pulling splinters from the hands of the clock,
plucking cobwebs from the hair of cruelty,
and understanding that the way the wind shifts a leaf
along the edge of the driveway is enough;
why do some need more?

as the stars of snow plummet through
the storm along the winter highway southbound,
your respite murmur is not forgotten, old friend,
the coldness of your beer and the kindness
of your words and gestures and silences
make all the difference,
and to know that you're still out there
makes the miles seem worth it
makes the bottles rattle
makes the trees think twice
about the winter gale
and it gives them courage to face it all head on
like a man of himself might do

Rampart

in the autumn I try to catch
the leaves as they fall from
the maples here on Rampart
Street but they slip by
like so many days and nights
and in the winter no one can park
here because it is too steep
and cars have slipped down the
hill right into traffic;
the spring rains flood
the yards toward
the bottom of the hill and
eat away at the gardens up top
but in the summertime you
can feel a breeze up here
so pure it almost seems untouched
by humanity, the distant lights
almost hum as they diamond
through the sky
and a cricket nearby keeps
the heartbeat of Rampart Street
in tune for another night,
another season, one
tumbling after the other infinite
until the cricket
and the breeze and the lights
and the rain and I are all gone to another
place altogether,

though it's not quite time
for that yet

Maybe a bird will sing

this style of living is madness,
running across boulevards to bars
unhinged from time and reality, mind spinning
from the liquor and the many beers, from
the thrumping trumpets of jazz nightclubs
and rotten gin joints named after long dead
poets and writers who never would have set foot
in such places for reasons they may disagree with
if exclaimed by modern hopeful usurpers of the night,
the written word outlaws, so plain and childish
in too aggressive a manner, forgetful
of where we're headed,
we need to look ahead as often as look back, and I ask:
where is the cemetery? the bones of our elders?
fed to dogs in a deep sleep, dreaming
of elderberry bushes across open fields,
far from sidewalks and human hands
and fingers and triggers and metal machines that
no animal understands or wants or cares for;
this style of living is madness, the way we run headlong
and blindfolded, the way the truncheons fly,
the way flies fly and screams fly choked on the politics
and religion and economy of our fables and lore
and all the while I think maybe a bird will sing
from a low enough branch for us to hear in time,
in time to pull our blindfolds loose,
in time to crawl to the grated window of our prison
and witness one more gust of life,
one more gift of sunlight, and then we will know
it is okay to be kind, even if it means goodbye

I hear the broken telephone...

lost in the shimmering awe
of Northern California,
birds pinwheel across the sky away and away

high on a hill from the top of San Francisco
skyscrapers watch and you will see
there is a docile acceptance
of a gilded age that has passed but still lives
in the blood of the streets;
nobody sees it, the massive churning of fate,
the dog collar, the leash, a long line of street vendors
selling fruit and newspapers that later tumble across
the cement slabs of furious America

"you can't get tequila unless you go through
Don Julio because Don Julio
is the ambassador
of tequila
in the United States"

the bartender seems to know what he's talking
about, but with an air
that is slender on faith and rich
in the eyes, hoping
that I will somehow support his rambling,
or maybe not, maybe I don't know anything,
I can't read these west coast faces
like the stolid New Englanders
who open so well in their most secret ways
that even they don't realize;
a game to play to pass the time till death

here it is different, here it is incandescent,
here I see that every level of every silver tower

hides a Gucci markdown of $2,012.00, and today only
we have high Hollywood oversight, dirt cheap, now
tilted northward and dyed platinum blond or auburn

depending on the season

there is a Gap on the corner of Haight/Ashbury
built by a fading generation lost to itself,
hopes browbeaten, history left dead
by those who carried it for so long;
it was too rotted to pick back up

there are no more Kerouacs, Keaseys, Thompsons
just painted buildings and neon signs,
neo-nazis with fleece vests and giant cell phones
ringing while passing empty phone booths;
everyone so eager to talk
the talk and curse
anyone who looks them in the eye

in the setting sun, in the dark,
people move into shells,
people run for cover,
there will be another false time,
there will be a worse time than this,
between New York and the Midwest and the Pacific
the downward spiral cannot be reversed,
everything we see and hear will be false
and grow even more false under the pretense
of liberty, of ethical seduction, of art and the importance
of saving everyone around us with our art, yet we cannot even
save ourselves for we lack
the willingness to be alone

it is so vital to know the power
of being alone

but in the streets shining with fruit vendors
and cable cars, it is possible to learn
this skill, it is possible to become a wave
within a wave sliding out
beneath a bridge into the sea
a bridge as red as the sun within our bursting capillary
dreams of America,
dreams unresolved yet still warm
still radiating hope
like the hills and streets
in the summer dusk of another lost night
in the great swaggering memory
of that distant, perfect San Francisco

Abate

as the heartbeat slows, so do the flames
throbbing in the fireplace across the
room from their couch, curled up alone
with the blanket they gave you; you
are contented with distant highway sounds,
Malibu coastal lullaby
in the November chill you never saw coming
in rolling golden California hill country,
memories of laughing together in a local coffee
shop, old friends fading away right before your eyes,
and later, in the dark, you sink, the fire low,
embers holding on,
this is the end, they whisper,
you'll never see these people again
and tomorrow there is a promise
only waves can keep, swelling deep, hinting loss
but always coming round again
for another chance

at dawn, embrace
as you walk across the sun-bleached
parking lot, you turn to see
they are already gone,
their bones and synapses replaced
by Pacific winds and mountain dust,
the passing silence speaks
for everything that should be said but
never will; the highway a canyon,
your time the burning
sun

It also rises

sometimes life gets so bad down there at
at the end of the rope that you feel almost
invincible, untouchable, cut free
from the hell that comes with Being,
and it's a little like freefalling,
exhilarating and terrifying, and these
moments usually come in that glowing hour before
dusk when the sun paints a yellow sheen
on the dust of the tenement, the sidewalk,
the parked and dented cars outside
the bars and laundry-mats
up and down Franklin Street

but at some point after the sun sinks
when you're walking home from the corner
market where you couldn't afford anything
more than two cans of tuna in light oil
your mind instinctually reaches out and discovers
there's still more rope to go before
the bottom—and that feeling isn't always a relief,
it can be even more terrifying than the one
that came before, the horror of knowing
that the fire still feeds

but buried beneath the nerves
and nausea and anxiety and
hopelessness there's also
a small voice that sometimes comes
in the latest hours of the night, a voice
telling you to go
to bed, that the rope will still
be there the next day
and you'll either climb it and ascend
into a more tolerable ring of Hell,

or you will fall trying, so
you go upstairs and open
a can of tuna
and eat it over the sink, turn off the light,
and lie in bed, willing your heart
to slow, maybe even stop
—but it won't, not yet

not quite yet

Cheapjack

they don't allow anyone to smoke indoors
anymore so we sit outside and drink
cheap whisky as he makes half-accurate quotes from
Shakespeare, Hunter Thompson, Hemingway,
even his own half-mad genius father,
that postal worker bingo player with the kindest
eyes and therefore the most beautiful,
but no matter the tale or ghost he attempts to conjure,
the reverie fades as the lights of the patio
dim to gold yellow halogen piss
glowing against stucco; we both know this feels
nothing like it used to, and later, walking
through the parking lot to the next bar, darker now,
a breeze suddenly comes on and it all lines up at once,
all his truth in a long peal of laughter, making the years
feel like seconds and ageless infinity; a comforting
cocoon of neon and cheap whiskey and shadows
across parking lots forever, his long black hair
catching the wind, my friend of age beyond age, both
of us smiling at the inescapable truth:
we have known each other too long to not be friends,
and not yet long enough for the gods to pay
any attention to what mayhem we may discover next

Dealing with the devil in the middle of the road

time is the sweetheart of my hell

no savior can burden this war
no relief comes at the light of dawn
there is a sense of failure when the lights go out

I have stopped staring into the light
I have slit the wrists in the wrong direction
the dreams will dry and heal in the dark
only for me to rise again, to hear a voice,
and feel the hours slip by like her summer rain

that's when I'll put down that knife
walk to the crossroads
and wait for my final ride to appear

The grass and dandelions and me

picnic table in the Virginia sunshine,
a highway rest break eyes closed bird
songs and cars in the distance washing
over the grass and dandelions and me

provisional waking, places to go

wind in the stratosphere, heartbeat,
heartbeat, fleeting dream-images
                              gone forever

lying on top of the picnic table,
listening to families
get in and out of cars, places to go

these proxy-war wanderings north
and south and back again, crossing
the Mississippi like stitching a wound,
it can take years, I know, to find
anything worth wandering for

they say it's the journey, not
the destination, and yet we
all have places to go

across the rolling fields roiling black
clouds move en masse toward me
and I wonder how many men and women
died in those fields, civil war treachery,
thinking of places and people so far
behind them, so far ahead, and the first
drop of rain stains the wooden picnic
table in silence, then three more

I feel one on my face and rise to walk
back to my car to accelerate forward
between white lines and studded shoulders
and black macadam until mile markers
begin their metronome dance with
the hours of my life, leading me to the
next unsure thing, places to go
always so many places to go
                              and then like that

            I'm gone forever

Footpath through the landmines

give me a phrase, a word with a simple line,
something only I know,
me, your vagrant translator

we have gone to waste over a night full of knots,
strings wisp and coil along your finger
pointing to the heart-mind
to the footpath through the landmines

the red string is for December
the blue one is for you
the green one holds tight to all the nights
when I couldn't drink enough
and there are too many white strings glowing
in the candlelight—those are for our
kinder memories drowning in shallow graves
and whispering in the dark

there is no helping the stains,
says the painter to the smock
there is no easing the calluses,
says the player of the viola
there is no stopping the swell,
says the rider of the waves

but I say, let the lines roll out on the page
and let them cut the strings,
let them fall into the riptide lapping
so they may wash out to sea, free, at last

Lions in the hallway

at times, the couch hums along with the heart
and unconsciousness melts to a stream,
a monologue of saved moments held and released;
the day-rush of the subway, the madness of the streets,
Miles Davis in the next room and red wine
glinting in the lamplight—real life filling a room
as Bird Parker blows, dissecting lonely memories
you have of trees in the Serengeti, lions in the hallway,
vultures circling over a fresh corpse
protected from the long November rains,
and when you close your eyes there are faces
in the music, there are dreams that make you cry—
these things soak into the walls
until no sound, not even
the police sirens clawing at the windows
can break through; there is only truth,
and wine, the eternal soul, and another
Blue Note record spinning to a stop

Set a course by a fading star

we spoke at great length about infidelity
the balance of desire tilting ahead of our pace;
this winter has failed to break
as April promised it would
and across the street, the church steeple bears witness,
hooded gray amid the crumbs of falling snow

nearing midnight, the weight of tomorrow
drapes over every aching moment;
you sleep like a child knowing full well the winter
blow outside will keep you home tomorrow, and I roam
the hallway outside the bedroom, knowing
soon my tracks in the snow will disappear as easy as
the lights of home on the wounded horizon

The ghosts of flat tires and dead flowers

shards of the setting sun
scatter across the wall and as I stare
from my floor they become the ghosts
of all the things that may yet consume me,
all the memories I cannot shake

the ghost that comes when I think
of my grandfather and his last dying
moments alone on his kitchen floor

the ghost of that long highway that led
from my father's house to the beach
and the way the sun would
shimmer all along the blacktop

the ghost of old roommates wronged
and the warm dust we left behind
when we agreed to part ways

the ghosts of flat tires and dead flowers

the ghosts of needles piercing veins
in the steady white light of the hospital

the ghost of unrequited love

the ghost of that ambulance ride
down San Pedro and
the ghost of my best friend smoking alone
in a bar that no longer exists

years and decades of them,
fading translucent and crossing blank walls,
empty spaces, my eyes closing against them

then opening to find my time unexpired,
the ages waiting, the ghosts silent

not yet haunting, only present

and so I pull on my shroud and go out
to sacrifice more of my days and nights
on the alter of time,

until the End comes for whatever I have left
and scatters me across that final
blood red sunset
where I'll join the ranks
of those blank spaces
fading against someone else wall,
at last

You get what you need

he said it felt too common to Google his ex
and discover she'd been arrested for prostitution in
South Dakota of all places, the Badlands,
as we trundled down the tilted steps
to the street in search of a quiet park that
doesn't seem to exist in lower Manhattan,
but coffee vans, they exist and
moor themselves to concrete islands
near subway stairs and newspaper boxes
and lines form, cops, delivery men with bikes,
women with strollers and expensive handbags,
the Rolling Stones blare flagrant from tin
radios spilling June heat onto the sidewalk
fifteen Manhattan streets converging on
one intersection, on one heart-riddled mind gasping
at the immensity of not the city, of not life or love, but
the way in which these moments come, when
for one minute every few months, things
align without leg-numbing meditation
or prayers to a godlike foolishness
and whether or not love is coming or going
or life will be okay or just continue to be
mediocre until death, everything is keyed in and firing
scintillating to the beat of the moment-world
because the line keeps moving, the sun keeps setting,
because the Rolling Stones are playing like fire
and if you try sometimes, you just might find

Polluted insomnia of the city

even the polluted insomnia of city
bus taxi subway neon yellow red lights
stop sign fast food sulfur eyes bleeding
breathing bludgeoning masses massing
cannot deter the need and craving
desire for the small set of stairs
to the small room where one can lay
in bed and watch the feet passing
the window during the day and watch
headlight ghosts corral the nightmares
of all your restless lifetimes once dark
falls along the streets and avenues of
grid-system depravity, dagger songs,
fervid incantations and stray metrocards
scattered like ticker tape parades for a
long lost youth, a hero's song, no more
heroes here only the faintest hint of radio
news, eyeglasses abandoned on the tracks,
a police presence on the platform,
heat and sweat and night wind now
coming down the small steps through the
small window into the room where
the lights are shot dead and dying, the
feet passing by, the rumble of what is
to come rocking you to sleep bringing
dreams from the gods, down to you,
asleep in the polluted insomnia of the city
and safe for now, just for now, amen

Four winds

1. Brooklyn waterline lapping at night,
the skyline lit like a gap-toothed smile;
the small change of my heart left behind
in all those island streets and taverns

2. as I wait for you to apologize to the bartender
and maybe get her number, I close my eyes
to the Texas night; it breathes; I breathe;
one day, neither of us will be here to remember

3. from the gas station I can see the Pacific
but I can't hear it, can't feel it or taste it, but
I can smell it, and a fragment shard of me like
glass is buried deep in that moment, so far away

4. as we move from one bar to the next, I stop
and look east and sense the pine trees and mountains
beyond these Albany lampposts and cobble; home
is a bone you cannot break, a midnight that never ends

You just don't know

like a boxer
meeting
his maker

like a broken
bottle cap half-hidden
beneath a shoe

like a stomach
three days
empty,
nothing but
air

like the last cloud
over El Paso
sinking in blue
waves
and knowing

like the death
of a cat

like a dust
mote
listless and going
south

like the
end of the last
song ever played
on the last
radio

like the onset of influenza

like the haunted silence
of an elevator
filled to capacity

like the worst
magician
just starting to warm
up

like a finger
without
a nail

like a stamp
without
glue
or a tongue

like a flower bent
by cruel tomboy fingers

like a sigh into
a phone without a voice
on the other end
to hear

like murder

like murder next
door

like a morning broken
by dogs barking
children crying
mowers mowing

sirens screaming
memories halting
kettles whistling
televisions blaring
glass shattering
or guns nearby

so when you hang up, or walk out the door, or even say
goodbye, smiling as you do, try to think
about all the things it is like the moment you
leave this small existence
of mine

Astral graveyard loneliness

robust twilight failures
sweep down like broken crows
when the moon ain't nowhere near
the window or the sky
no north star marker to guide the worn and weary
back to bed

what light is left when your own fire dies?
when the days stand like headstones?
when the nights go white with memories?

somewhere downstairs a telephone explodes
a bloom of hate against a sleepless mind;
everyone wants something, but nothing
that matters, nothing that will last beyond
a headstone or two, a few numbers
on a stone wall—that's all

the blankets are old friends
worn thin with favors,
the pillows browned by
nightmares, stained spittle-gray;
unwanted by any other, I keep them
like horded fool's gold, mine forever

the curtains are open
showing no moon skies
astral graveyard loneliness,
I forgive the moon;
we all need a break from the full
view of humanity from time to time
and I can only hope it will come back
and forgive me,
please, please forgive me

Another small feeling on another small night

your bones will grow
accustomed to the ballast of the night

this pain feels like it will never end
and in a way it never will

you say,

this is *you*: the ringing silence
in your ears

the bones of your back contort into
a knife, a knife so cold and sharp

this *is* you,
you think,

and this is all you can take after
everything else you have had to carry all these years

you say,

maybe the candle will blow itself out while you fall;
no more pain if you want it

You don't have to go home but you can't stay here

the long, aching descent into midnight
guided by neon bar lights reflecting
off the whiskey and gin bottles lining
the mirror, our reflections blocked,
the doorways and exits blocked, the cries
of the innocent outside muted by the last
of our collective quarters in the jukebox
playing out the gutter hymns that will
never save our souls but at least sooth
the pain we feel when raising our glasses
to indicate we'd like another, please,
just one more before we close our eyes
to the darkness of the lights going out
one by one until we navigate by pure
desire alone, my last friend in this realm
whispering beside me how glad he was
to know he'd finally go where she
might be waiting for him, but I do not
reply, it already happened, we have risen
and fallen at once, glasses emptying
in a last eucharist gesture,
our sins needing no forgiveness,
just the darkness within the dark,
the endless shades of night,
where even creation becomes a myth
and the memory of neon reflections
the only religion that matters

Waiting on Rocky

Rocky's pub in San Francisco
opens early at 9 a.m.
but to get there was the worst
chore imaginable,
8 hours on a bus from North Hollywood
with all the other lost and weary souls,
myself included, all sweating the same color,
the same sex, the same poverty, the
same desire in the same heat,
the air conditioner busted and the john
three rows back reeking heavily
of refuse,
the sun hell bent plowed down on us
from just above the Pacific,
never sinking, never dying, always murder
and getting off that bus was a godsend that
even the goth kids at the club
next door to the greyhound station
couldn't diminish or paint away with black,
but it was too late in San Francisco
and no hotel would have me,
some tech conference
eating up all the good and even
the cheap rooms,
so I camped it behind a dumpster
near the Ashbury Cleaners,
sober, sunburned, heartbroken, wanting
to die peacefully in a women's arms
or at least drinking one last glass of whiskey
and I somehow made it to 9 a.m.
when a real Irishman opened the door and made
the best bloody mary I ever had,
curing all ills for one more day
a miracle I never could've imagined

all those years ago as an abstinent snob;
you see, vagrancy has a habit
of sweetening the pot of life
in ways that morning eyes and a diamond
ring just never could,
but diamonds die hard and so do I,
and so does the morning light
shining across the bay of this beautiful city
that I hope will never
slip into the sea
though we all must
eventually

The gargoyle crew gets ready for another night in hell

they were stoic gargoyles
in the cool of the kitchen
before it all went to nightly hell
white jackets and towels stained
with blood and grease and sweat
and they knew every name of
every region of France, every kind
of oyster in the fridge, every
cut of beef known to mankind
and nobody could hear us down there
in the basement beneath their tables
where we swore and laughed
and called out orders or demands
for drinks and more meat or fish
which is where I came in, leaving
my pots and pans in the sink
to fetch them whatever they needed
knowing I would get a snippet
of respect in return, a grain of sand
that might add up to something someday,
and when I'd come back they'd call
out and ask, *what song is this?*
Jeremy always slipping in some new
mix CD he made the night before
or a bootleg Clash live recording from NYC
and sometimes it was some deep cut
I'd never know in a million years,
thinking it yet another *Black Market Clash*
B-side but no, an earlier 101'ers tune,
get it right, rookie! they'd shout, but then
easy ones would come to me, and
I was always surprised when they thought
I didn't know Dire Straits' "Six Blade Knife"
or Zeppelin's "Kashmir" or

the opening notes of "Blue in Green" by
the savior of all souls Miles Davis
ending our nights with endless jazz
as we scrubbed the floors and the bottoms
of copper pots, knives, ladles,
our hands raw and bodies stinking
stumbling to cars like zombies back
from a life we'd lead again tomorrow

but being young, other things
became more important,
like going to New Year's Eve
parties and skipping shifts, leaving them
fucked so bad they wouldn't speak to me
again when I went in two more times before
blowing that job for the next one, and the next,
and all the ones to follow, feeling bad
for failing Jeremy and Bryan our chef, who
knew every bass player by name as he knew
every sort of fish in the sea, and it was
a long time before I thought of sad-faced Bryan
and his dream to own his own restaurant

years later when I walked down a pier in California
as the sun set low against the water and
"Six Blade Knife" came from a nearby boombox and
it all came back, everything I learned and lost
and fumbled away, the respect and the time
pissed down dive bar drains, Bryan and his smile
when I finally figured out the difference
between crimini and shiitake mushrooms,
between cod and pollock and tilapia, between shit beer
and good beer and how after a certain
point in the night it doesn't matter anymore;
and I hope he's still out there, maybe not hustling
as much but easing into his own restaurant's
back door to watch his gargoyle crew get ready

for another night in hell, in heat, in music,
in the weeds as some other young punk with no
idea how to tell the difference between Husker
fucking Du and the Replacements screws up
a run for fish from the walk-in fridge, and maybe
in that moment he'll think of me, but not likely
since we all fade in sunsets and reappear ages
away on shores forever unfamiliar and new,
until even the sun tires and turns away for good

Where now, Li Bai?

some of us scream because we are going
insane, or are insane, or can only hope
to go insane because no other solution
exists for the torn thumbnail of our lives

from each crow-lined wire whispers
solemn hums of primordial hope;
if all the world took a sick day,
not a soul would be heard from again

the sun rising is the weepless bane
of our existence; we give away our time,
hand away our relevance, our recognition that
we are wasting away, for what?

once rivers ran unheard, oceans swelled unseen
once the mountains told stories to the plains
about the kingdom of clouds, the land of rain
and how each drop lived a lifetime as it fell

each blade of grass sings in the summer wind,
but none of us can hear the song; we lost
the moon before we knew the moon was ours,
and now we listen to wolves howl in misery

in tune to the empty hands of humankind

Elliott Road

bright summer spigots
and crickets chirping fire
across the lukewarm nights
that jackspring through
tall grass suburbia
where power lines cut wrists
against the grain of clouds
and moons and sunsets,
turning blue skies orange then
red and purple and dead

sometimes my cuts dry and stick
to my clothes but it takes a while

sometimes the medicines makes me
dizzy and sick all the next day

sometimes the shadows creep along
the dandelions, edging deeper
into life, past the days, past the weeks,
past the cracks along the road near
the mailbox and out into the years
and decades and so far down the road
that looking back to see yourself
sitting in that cherry tree in your grandfather's
front yard becomes so hard, too hard

and now, that house is no longer painted white,
the cherry tree gone, the pool filled in,
and the road keeps going, crickets chirping,
fire rising throughout the lukewarm nights

and the blood beating in your heart
is red and purple and one day dead

one day, you think, one day

as the moon and clouds hover
and you steadily
march away from the sunset horizon
of your youth

Stray
(for Mike Belardi)

my friend, your little bungalow beneath
the palm trees of San Antonio
was the oasis I needed during a hell storm
of endless blues;
your chess set and stereo
saved me so often that I'll never
be able to repay you,
not with all the pearls from the sea
or the golden shimmering miles that separate
us yet, but they won't forever,
I promise

Slaves of some strange god

from the elevated subway platform you
can see the street below full of garbage
and potholes and generations working
so they can keep on working ten years
from now, and ten hundred years after
that, supposing we all live to see
the next train come barreling up, sweeping
the stink high and wafting through
our legs and arms and spaces between
our solitary crowded stance

in evenings after shoes and clothes find
the floor and bourbon finds the heart we
lay inside and listen to the sun sink out there,
fade into some far away sea where nobody
knows the trouble we've seen, and nobody
knows our sorrow

there will be awful nights when you cannot sleep,
your life, your guts will twist up around
your sides and neck, your legs and swollen feet,
feeling sick, nausea rippling the sheets
and the bed is hot to the touch like fever

and I believe that you, like me, suffer so

no pillows or sheets bring comfort
no totems or wishes or memories
will bring us the things we want,
the people we need—it only brings us
the people we don't
and the midnights we cannot escape

look around the room now, isn't it true

that our days are only the decorations
of a tomb? I wish only for total silence,
for slaves of some strange god to brick up
the doors and windows and train tunnels
all around this room, create a dark respite,
a timeless unknown that pulls and chews
on our bones, cursed by our own sickness,
all of us just lint left behind by the ageless ages

bring me that; there's nothing else to bring
unless you bring morning, in which case I agree,
let us rise and see
what hell or life-saving love
might come next

Jazz is dead

jazz is dead, bop, cool, all of it,
and every so-called jazz
joint in New York City seems to hang a sign
of reeking death and disease out front,
prophesizing great shows within
for cover charges that no honest bum or
jazz lover can afford, because jazz
does not know money, and the moneyed
cannot know jazz, because jazz
spends too much time drinking behind the club
with blues and too much time dancing in the basement
with swing, long forgotten swing—beautiful
spinning dresses and white jacket swing;
jazz is not a regal affair; jazz is sweat with style,
crazed feet jabbing at the floor, exhaled everything
clouding a small room packed with the lowdown
miners of the soul, and sometimes jazz is death alone,
stone silent in a room with rotgut wine
and cigarette smoke streaming
through a dime-store radio,
the soundtrack of a love-derailed train,
a mass-murdered heart,
there is no cover charge to watch a man die
beside his radio, is there? there is no cover charge
to hang down in the alley with the other nighthawks,
is there? where is this, the Bowery? Hell's Kitchen?
I can no longer tell, yet there they are, you can see
them through the door, getting ready to play
in their suits, men and woman sitting at little tables
waiting, hands folded, and the man at the door
with a red box ready for the money, a stoic
bartender with a row of perfectly polished glasses,
it's all through that door, all waiting for you,
but not you, per say

but a better you, a better dressed you,
a better paid you, they want to show you
the carcass of a great beast that once
roamed free and wild,
soothing the wounds of a mob of
lonesome aching lovers striving
to hold on to the night
just long enough to say they felt
the world breathe at least once more
—a deep inhale before the long blow
of death's improvisation

Panhandle nocturne

sit and swing,
listen
to the ghosts
ringing out the wind-chime song
across the prairie dusk

in time, the clouds will roll in,
form your contour

they do not age, only deepen

close your eyes on the wide wooden porch
and feel the air hum low to the horizon

as your spider-numb hand holds tight
to a red-dappled Roman apple, waiting

the chimes, the ghosts, the feathered grasslands
hold their breath in the summer wind

and then, along the distance,
the dirt roils

and you see the truth

the ghosts were right: this day will end us
before it ends itself

and there isn't much time now,
but there's still time

to breathe deep, and if you're able,
remember

Ubiquitous
(for Jesse Cruz)

1. the wavering effect of one's voice
when reminiscing about the time
we all lived together in a small second floor
apartment, the two of you
taking the bedroom and pretending not to be
married at work because you'd both lose
your job if they found out
that the assistant manager was dating
one of the dancers,
and me on the couch,
the dark nights spent drinking the cheapest
beer we could afford on minimum wage

2. the look in one's eyes when thinking back
to crickets chirping in urban heatwave midnights
and the time we came back
from the pool hall to find she had cleaned
your entire apartment
top to bottom
out of love
but all those empty whiskey bottles were gone
and the giant bowl of cigarette stubs
that you had kept
on your coffee table
it was gone too, and she dared you
to complain,
and later she filled your kitchen
with black and white cow patterns and she always
wanted a hug when either of us left the apartment,
in case it was the last time we saw each other,
this wonderful outspoken my-way-or-highway being,
this suntanned spirit, the biggest soul
we'd ever meet, how you two fell apart down south

not long after we parted way
        and then she fell to cancer

later on we drank about it, and later on I got cancer too
but made it through, and now I sit alone
many nights and I think of you
working oil rigs
chainsmoking one midnight away after another
your life drifting into the sky
curling gray and silver, and it sounds so sentimental
and so stupid but now and then
I worry I'll never see you again
I don't want to be the only one left
to walk these streets at night
thinking about how dumb lucky happy we were
back in those early apartment days
back in those cold New York winters
or south Texas heat-wave mid-night bar-crawls
because when you go, it won't be something
I can drink away
and it makes me feel feeble and soft
just thinking about it coming on the horizon, but
we're getting there, and I want
a few more neon bar nights with you
to make sure I remember it right,
to laugh about how you'll outlive us all,
to pitch empty bottles
into the tall grass and howl
like it was all yesterday, just a few more times,
just once more, and then I promise
I'll turn the lights out and lock that door
when I leave the apartment
to go walk the night,
never minding where, just go,
full dark with all those stars
blinking for the three of us somewhere
bright and new

Good and honest and true

I harbor a great sadness for this world. I feel us pulling away from sanity like layers of onion skin, delicate at first, then thicker and deeper, stinging the eyes, pungent, poison, and I want to cry but it feels hopeless to cry and so I stare into the dark at the stars hidden by electric night and I try to forget who I'm supposed to hate and how much I'm supposed to want and how proud I'm supposed to be about something that won't matter once this great hulking planet of stone and water and lava suicides at last in order to rid itself of us for good. I worry about the fighting and the killing over what little we haven't tainted. I worry about my siblings and their children. I worry over the idea that no one with the power to stop it cares enough because they will all be gone by the end—and it is coming, it is close. It feels useless, and yet here we are, here I am. I harbor a great sadness that this is all for nothing. But while it still means something, if only to us, I want to hold tight to you and be as good and honest and true as I can. I hope you are there with me looking up that those fading stars at night, hoping for the same. But no matter where you are, I will be there thinking of you and all this, tending what I can until then end. I promise.

A long stretch of empty highway

this is a long stretch of empty highway
but I don't always know where I am

often it's that quiet part of Texas between
the city and the coast where only
the most distant lights come into view
from ranches or small rest-stops beyond
the fields of cotton or stubble, or

it's the California emptiness, inching
northward along the endless dry valley
in the middle of nowhere, the dash lights
of the bus glowing green as we collectively
sway in the dark of the night, or

it's somewhere circling Albany, stitching
through local exit ramps and bridges,
downtown blocks and suburban
sprawl connecting all the municipalities
of a youth out of reach and a death
whispering through the stereo, which

plays that mix CD I made so many
years ago, the tracks by Miles Davis
nearing midnight and Jack
Kerouac reading his poetry into the
void of tomorrow and more tomorrows
he never dreamed of, and

as I listen I grip the wheel and
stare out into the night, the stripes
on the road, the double yellow line, red
lights and street lights and neon dancing
in the pools of rain along the shoulder as

the music reels into the night,
the soft words moaning through lips
now dust, from a mind now wind, from
a soul now part of our souls, here on
a Tuesday Friday Someday night

no matter when or where in this life
the road keeps going, and going,
the light and the dark and the march
of time, and when the hands
leave the wheel and the eyes close
and the highway ends, it will all
continue on without us, reset for
someone new, the entry ramp to the
highway glistening with fresh rain as
the headlights lead the way, Jack
leaning forward toward the microphone
and Miles is there too with his long
deep inhale for the next improvisation

and it will be perfect, and there will be peace,
just like that, just you wait and see

The last tree at Golden Gate

there is a single tree on the hill
where they once hung
irascible men in the old west
high overlooking Alcatraz
earthen heartache
and red clay desire
set adrift on
gold tan water skin, the genius of water
and the love of calm observation
solemn observation through silver
coin-operated viewers
to see a painted bridge on infinite repeat
once finished, again to start
and the last tree at Golden Gate
waits with one power line in sight
just to the right down the hill
where laborers work the harbor 'till dusk
stiff backs bred in Taiwan and Oklahoma
ground-down souls with hats, trucks, homes
and worries unknown to the wind
that ruffles the feathers in the last tree
at Golden Gate

All I know of karma

let's hop trains, you say
run away to the west like children
as I stand over the deep end
on the diving board holding champagne at 9 a.m.
the sky is the water below and the shimmering
above me is flush with simple transient movement
as a single brown
lifeless
leaf
dry like a Buddhist parchment
skitters toward the edge and holds
the concrete like my toes hanging over
the diving board

born of the east and knowing
all I know of karma
I would dive into the deep head first
but
the leaf holds in the wind, so
I cannot fail my life
with so much beauty left to fight for

Blue sky in the morning and nothing to do

I passed seven people jogging
on my way to get bacon and coffee
before going back to my small two
room apartment to take a nap and keep on
doing whatever it is we're all
doing before we get pulled under
        one by one
  and I don't think I'll be able
to do that, jog 10 miles
or swim 100 laps or any of that again;
they seem happy, they endure;
it's a good thing to be
but when I get down on myself about
not being able to do the things
I used to be able to do
I remind myself how I once

drank chemotherapy for six months
and kept on going

ate even more poison for years
and kept on going

swam beyond the sandbars in south Texas
and watched sharks dart beneath me
and kept on going

changed a flat tire 38 miles from anywhere
while rattlesnakes watched
from the shoulder of the highway and
kept on going

ate a hamburger on the side of a dirt road
in the canyons above LA and watched

a train cross a bridge glinting like
silver in the California sun
and kept on going

threw up from the wrong combination
of pills because I was a doctor's
guinea pig and kept on going

took three punches to the face once
and laughed at each of them and
kept on going

watched a ghost as it crossed the room
in my friend's kitchen in Alabama
and kept on going

stared at the stars above west Texas at an observatory,
knowing I'd dream of it forever,
and kept on going

helped my grandmother out of the tub when
she fell alone and crying at 2 a.m.,
both arms broken, heart broken,
just weeks before she finally died and I
kept on going

stared into sinks and tubs and toilet bowls
of blood and I kept on going

drank orange juice while still drunk
at a yacht club in San Rafael
with three rich strangers
I met the night before and almost fell into the
water but I didn't and I kept on going

convinced a sobbing rich guy the same night before
not to kill himself just because his

wife was cheating on him and he relented
and we both kept on going

watched a butterfly disappear into my chest
in the woods outside of San Antonio
and kept on going

watched towers fall and kept on going

watched demons feast and kept on going

watched a con-man fool my parents and kept on going

held hands with a stranger crying
on a park bench in NYC and kept on going

closed my eyes to the blue sky above
and felt the perfect breeze wash over me in the most
wonderful moment of my life and kept on going

watched Humphrey Bogart in *Sahara* firing
a machine gun at Nazis and kept on going

opened unread emails from friends who had earlier killed
themselves and kept on going

held my dying dog while we both lied on the floor
one last time and kept on going

drank until I needed someone to help
me home too often and kept on going, but drank
less so after that one night at Hemingway's

held newborn babies who were not my own
and cried later at how good it felt
and kept on going

stood next to casket after casket and kept
on going

got up from the pavement after a truck ran me down
in Austin, TX, brushed myself off, picked
up my cigarette, and I
kept on going

walked miles of empty Adirondack
roadsides picking wildflowers for no one
and kept on going

rejected love and was rejected by love and kept on going

found love and kept on going

ate bacon and drank coffee and passed beautiful
happy healthy joggers on my walk home
and kept on going until I got there
and sat on the front steps and thought about
all the wonderful terrible places and people
and things I've seen and experienced
and I hope I keep on going, but even if I
don't, this has been enough
and this has been worth it, blue sky
in the morning and nothing to do
but keep on going

Author Bios

J. Lester Allen lives in the sleepy waterfall holler of Ludlowville, NY. He is the author of three other collections of poetry, most notably *This Is a Land of Wolves Now* (Kung Fu Treachery, 2019).

James H Duncan is the editor of *Hobo Camp Review* and the author of such books as *We Are All Terminal But This Exit Is Mine*, *Nights Without Rain*, and *Vacancy*. He resides on a somnolent, tree-lined street in upstate New York. For more, visit www.jameshduncan.com.

www.ingramcontent.com/pod-product-compliance
Lightning Source LLC
Chambersburg PA
CBHW032042040426
42449CB00007B/979